DISCOVER AND DO!

SOUND

Written by Jane Lacey

Enslow PUBLISHING

Published in 2023 by Enslow Publishing, LLC
29 East 21st Street, New York, NY 10010

Editor: Katie Dicker
Designer: Clare Nicholas
Series Designer: Rocket Design (East Anglia) Ltd

Manufactured in the United States of America

CPSIA compliance information: Batch #CSENS23: For further information contact
Enslow Publishing LLC, New York, New York at 1-800-398-2504.

Please visit our website, www.enslowpublishing.com. For a free color catalog of all our high-quality books,
call toll free 1-800-398-2504 or fax 1-877-980-4454.

Cataloging-in-Publication Data

Names: Lacey, Jane.

Title: Sound / Jane Lacey.

Description: New York : Enslow Publishing, 2023. | Series: Discover and do! | Includes glossary and index.

Identifiers: ISBN 9781978530782 (pbk.) | ISBN 9781978530805 (library bound) | ISBN 9781978530799 (6pack) | ISBN 9781978530812 (ebook)

Subjects: LCSH: Sound--Juvenile literature. | Hearing--Juvenile literature.

Classification: LCC QC225.5 L334 2023 | DDC 534--dc23

Picture credits:

t=top b=bottom m=middle l=left r=right

Shutterstock: Panda Vector cover/title page l, serazetdinov cover/title page r, miniaria 4 and 22b, MSSA 4 and 22b, Abscent 5tr and 18t, tinkivinki 5br, 23t and 31m, drawkman 6t and 28, Iconic Bestiary 6b and 26b, Boyko.Pictures 6b and 8b, petovarga 7t and 7b, Ihor Biliavskyi 7b, Dhana Design 10t, Rain Art 10b, VikiVector 10br, Zaie 11t, mejorana 12t and 29t, alaik_azizi 12b, Dreamcreation 12b, Oguz Aral 14br, Number 86 14bl, Gaidamashchuk 16b, Rustic 16b, Natali Snailcat 18b, Kapitosh 18m, Oleksandr Derevianko 19t, Yuriy2012 20b, Jiripravda 22t, NotionPic 24t, Lyudochka 24b, Viktorija Reuta 25t, Serorion 26t, marina_ua 27t, Golden Sikorka 27mt, gokcen gulenc 27mb, Petrovic Igor 27b and 31t; Getty: vladwel 5tl, 7t and 31b, gmast3r 7b, MatoomMi 8t, Ilyaf 11t, jesadaphorn 14t, DenPotisev 16t and 30t, TopVectors 19t, urbazon 20t and 32, Aleutie 24b, 29b and 30b.

All design elements from Shutterstock.

Craft models from a previous series by Q2AMedia.

DISCOVER AND DO!

SOUND

Written by Jane Lacey

Enslow PUBLISHING

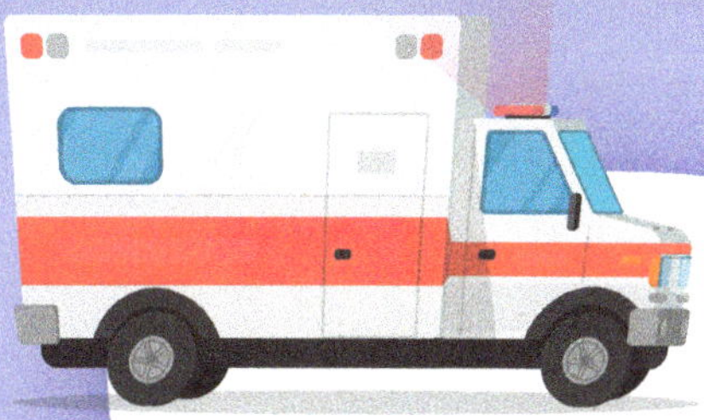

CONTENTS

Words that appear in **bold** can be found in the glossary on pages 28–29.

SOUNDS AROUND US

The world we live in is full of sound–people talking, traffic roaring, birds singing, and music playing. All these sounds give us information about what is going on around us.

The sound of a rooster crowing in the morning is a sign that the sun is rising.

Voices

Sounds help us to **communicate** with each other. We hear the sound of each other's voices when we talk. We hear our teacher at school giving us information and instructions and asking us questions.

These students are listening to their teacher talking to understand his instructions.

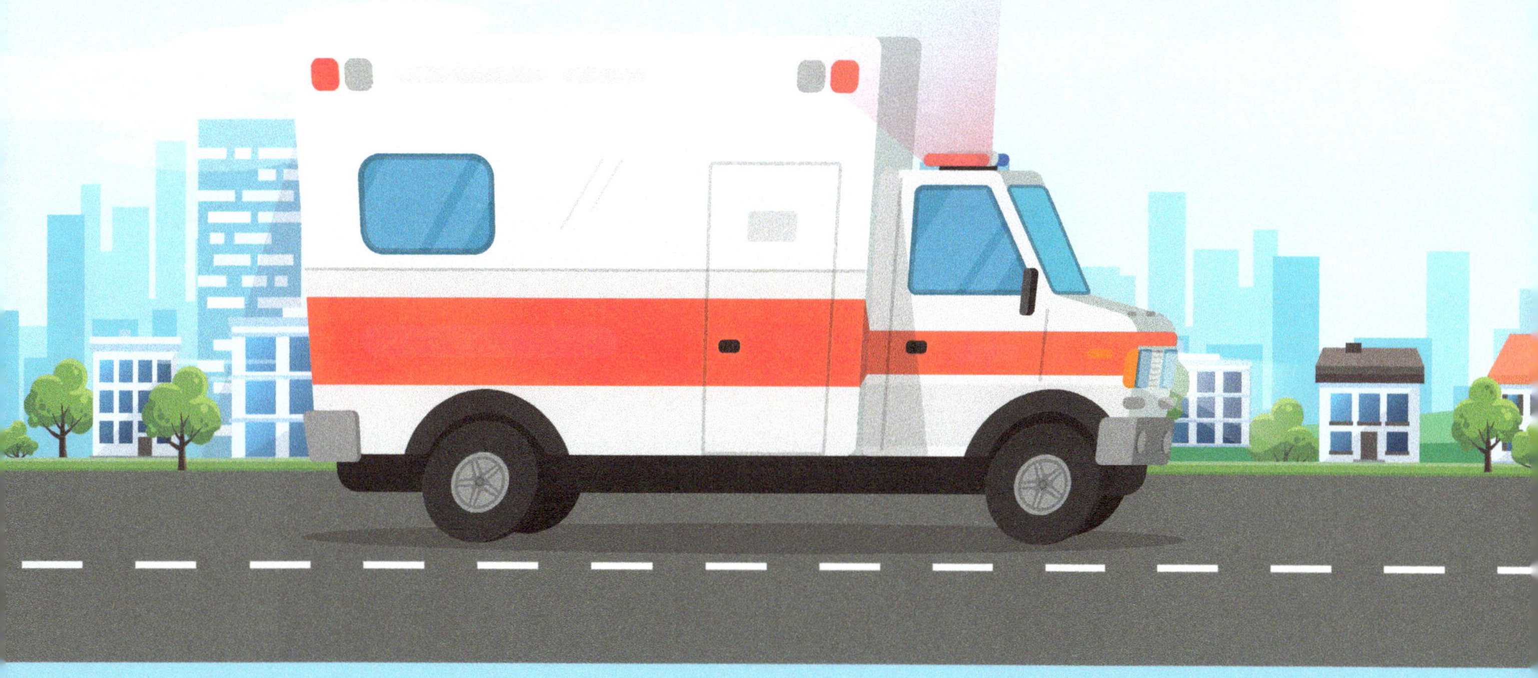

Danger!

Sounds warn us of danger. We listen for the sound of traffic before we cross the road. The school fire alarm warns us to get out of the building to safety. A fierce dog growls and warns us to keep away!

Entertainment

Some sounds entertain us. We hear voices and sound effects on the radio, television, at the theater, and at the movies. We enjoy listening to music and singing or playing a musical instrument to create sounds ourselves.

VIBRATIONS

Sounds are made when something moves and makes vibrations. These are very tiny movements to and fro that make sound waves in the air.

At a playground, children make loud sounds by shouting and laughing.

Moving

Big vibrations make loud sounds and small vibrations make quiet sounds. When you sit very still and whisper, you make quiet sounds because the air around you only vibrates a little. When you stamp your feet and shout, you make bigger vibrations.

Feeling sound

You can sometimes feel sound. If you put your hand on a radio playing loud music, you can feel the vibrations. Put your hand on your throat when you talk, laugh or sing, and you will feel your **vocal cords** vibrate.

When you sing, your vocal cords vibrate the air in your throat to make a sound.

When you pluck the strings of an instrument, they vibrate the air around them to make a sound.

ACTIVITY

MAKE A SOUND CANNON

Ask an adult to help you with this activity.

You will need:

- **rectangle of thin cardboard about 15 inches x 10 inches (38 cm x 25 cm)**
- **extra cardboard**
- **tape**
- **markers**
- **plastic from a sandwich bag**
- **scissors**
- **square of tissue paper**

1. Roll the cardboard into a tube and tape it together to make a cannon shape. Decorate your cannon with markers. Stretch the plastic tightly over one end of the tube and tape it in place.

2. Cut out a cardboard circle the same size as the end of the tube. Ask an adult to help you cut a small circle in the middle of it. Tape it over the open end of the tube.

3. Cut one side of the tissue paper to make a fringe. Ask a friend to hold the tissue fringe in front of the hole in the cannon.

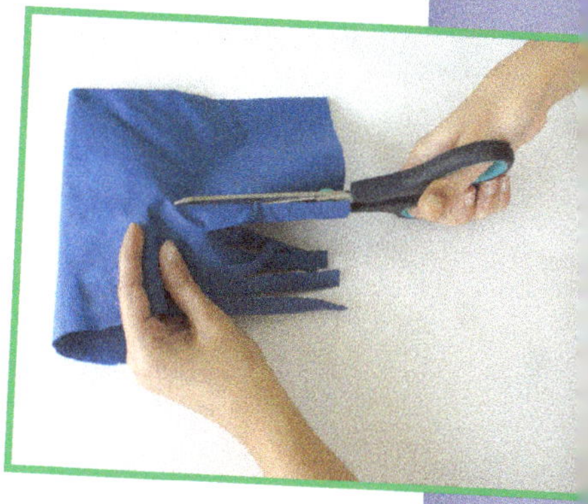

4. Tap the plastic at the other end of the cannon. Watch as the tap vibrates the air and makes sound waves that travel down the cannon and force air out of the hole, moving the tissue.

MOVING SOUND

When something moves, it makes vibrations that push against the **molecules** in **solids**, **liquids**, and **gases** so they vibrate too. This creates sound waves. Sound needs to travel through a solid, liquid, or gas for us to hear it.

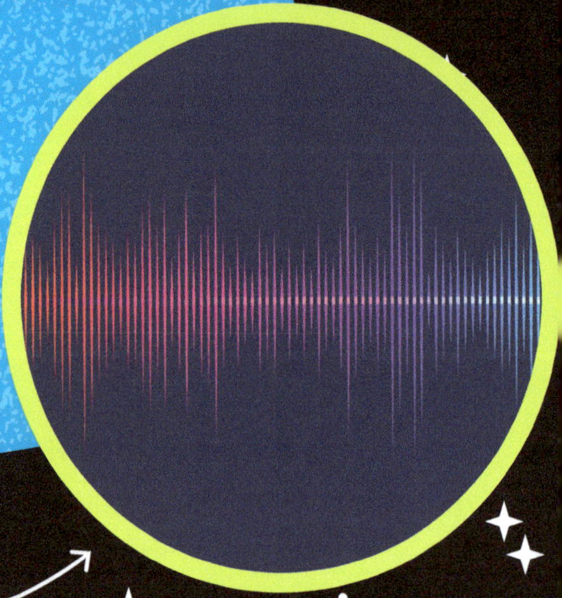

Scientists can measure the vibrations in sound waves.

Sound does not travel in space, so astronauts use radios to communicate.

Silence

There is silence when sound has nothing to travel through. Silence means there is no sound. It is silent in space, for example, because there is no air in space for sound to travel through. In contrast, planet Earth is surrounded by air that is full of sounds.

Fast and slow

Sound travels about four times faster through water than through air. Water molecules are close together so they pass on vibrations quickly. Underwater animals use sound to send messages to each other through the water.

Blue whales can communicate with other whales more than 500 miles (804 km) away.

ACTIVITY

LISTEN UP!

You will need:

- **3 plastic sandwich bags**
- **water**
- **sand**
- **pencil**

1. Fill the first bag 3/4 full with water. Fill the second bag 3/4 full with sand. Blow air into about 3/4 of the third bag. Fasten securely.

2. Put the bags onto a table. Put your ear to each bag in turn, while you tap the table with a pencil.

3. Through which bag did you hear the tapping sound most clearly? Make a chart to record your findings.

Try filling additional bags with other materials, such as tissues or cooking oil. How do these materials affect the tapping sound?

MAKING SOUNDS

You can make all kinds of different sounds by moving your body. You can use your voice to whisper, talk, sing, and shout. You can clap your hands and stomp your feet.

Maracas are filled with beans or beads. They rattle when you shake them.

Shaking and rattling

Shaking moves small objects inside a container or rattles objects together to make a noise. A baby's rattle makes a noise when the baby shakes it. Maracas are rattles that are shaken in time to music.

Tapping and banging

Tapping and banging two objects together makes a sound. A door knocker bangs against the door. A drummer bangs a drum with drumsticks. A bell clapper hits the side of a bell to make it ring.

You can make different sounds by banging a drum, tapping a gong, and clashing cymbals together.

ACTIVITY

MAKE A TAMBOURINE

You will need:

- **2 paper plates**
- **hole puncher**
- **buttons and beads**
- **colored yarn or ribbon**
- **pens or paints (or colored paper and glue)**
- **foil, bottle tops, or paper clips**

1. Put the plates together and punch holes around the rims about 0.75 inch (2 cm) apart.

2. Separate the plates and put some buttons and beads on one plate.

3. Turn over the second plate. Put it over the first and line up the holes, so the bottom side of each plate is facing outwards. Put the yarn or ribbon through the holes and tie the ends so the plates are held closely together.

4. Color the outer rim with pens or paints (or glue on some colored shapes). You could also tie anything that jangles and rattles to the holes–bits of foil, bottle tops, or paper clips.

Bang, rattle, and shake your tambourine!

HEARING SOUNDS

We have two ears, one on either side of our head. Our ears are the parts of our body we hear with. When sound waves travel into our ears, we hear the vibrations as a noise.

If you cup your hand around your ear to make your ear bigger, you can hear quiet sounds more clearly.

Ears

The parts of our ears that we can see are called outer ears or ear flaps. They are shaped like a cup to catch sound waves. Our inner ears are the parts of our ears we cannot see. They are made up of small, delicate parts.

How our ears work

Sound waves travel along the **ear canal** and make the **eardrum** vibrate. Three tiny ear bones carry the vibrations to the **cochlea**, which contains liquid. The vibrations travel through the liquid, then on to the brain as sound signals.

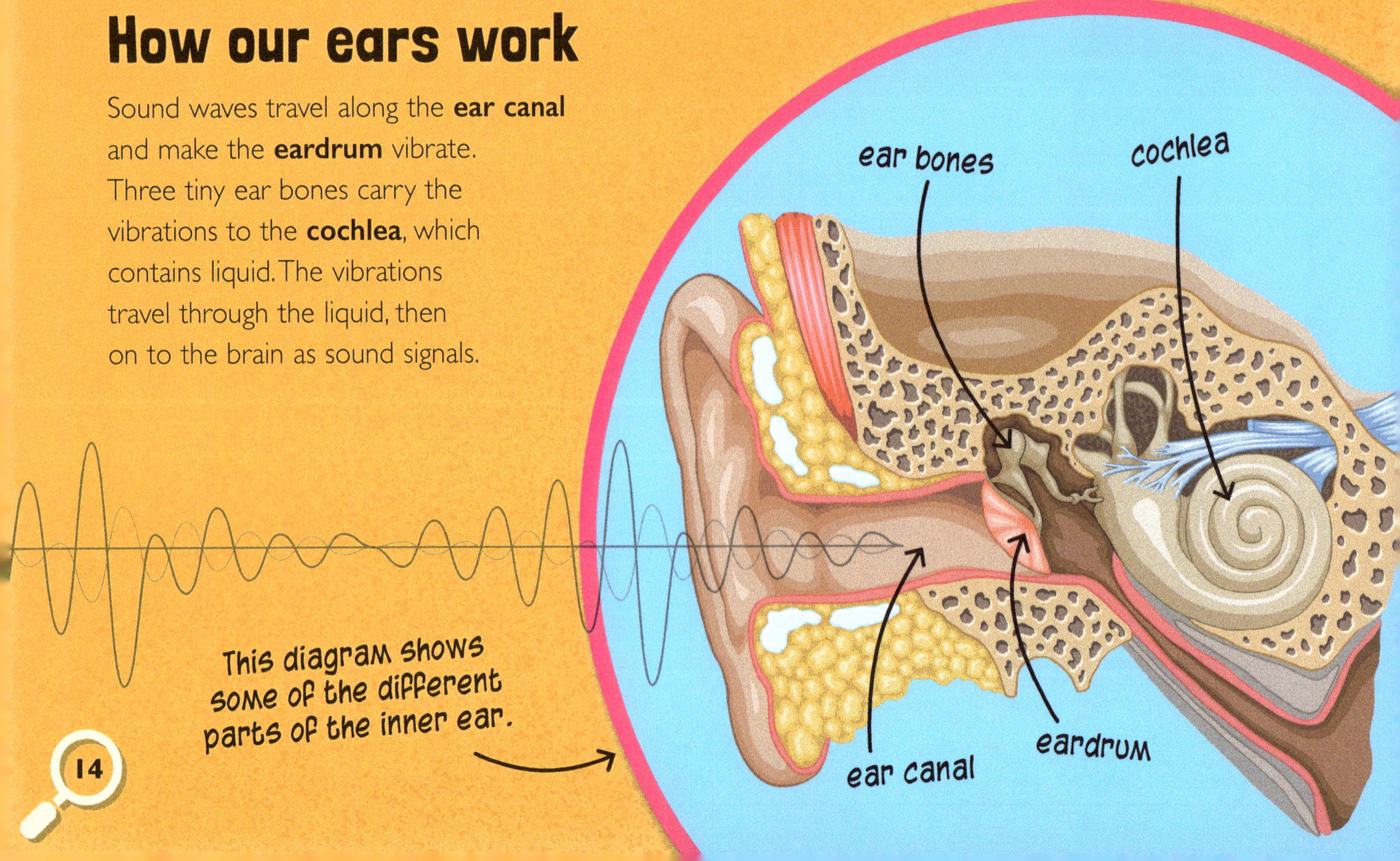

This diagram shows some of the different parts of the inner ear.

ACTIVITY

MAKE A MODEL EAR

Ask an adult to help you with this activity.

You will need:

- **foil pan about 8 inches x 4 inches x 2.5 inches (20 cm x 10 cm x 6 cm)**
- **scissors**
- **plastic food wrap**
- **tape**
- **bendable drinking straw**
- **ping-pong ball**
- **bowl of water**

1. To make the eardrum, ask an adult to help you cut a hole in the base of the foil pan, about the size of the rim of a mug. Stretch the plastic wrap over the top of the foil tray and tape it in place.

2. For the ear bones, cut both ends of the drinking straw with scissors to make flaps.

3. Tape the flaps of the bendy end of the straw to the ping-pong ball and tape the flaps of the other end of the straw to the middle of the plastic wrap.

4. The cochlea is the bowl of water. Rest the ping-pong ball on the surface of the water.

5. Speak through the hole in the base of the tray. Watch vibrations travel through all the parts of the ear and make ripples in the water.

ANIMAL HEARING

Some animals have very sharp hearing. They can hear a wider range of sounds than we can because they have specially adapted ears. They use their ears to find food or to escape from danger.

Hunters and hunted

Animals that are **predators**, such as foxes, and animals that are **prey**, such as rabbits, have big outer ears to collect the smallest sounds. Their ears can swivel to help them work out where the sound is coming from.

Amazing hearing

Bats hunt at night and use sound to catch moths for their food. They make very high squeaks and clicks. These sounds bounce off their prey and travel back as **echoes**. The echoes help the bat to figure out where the moths are flying.

ACTIVITY

MAKE AN EAR TRUMPET

An ear trumpet is used as a hearing aid. It is shaped like a cone and helps to direct sounds into the ear.

You will need:

- **sheet of card stock**
- **pencil**
- **string**
- **scissors**
- **tape**
- **strip of card stock**
- **pens or paints (or colored paper and glue)**

1. Draw a large semi-circle on the card stock and cut it out. To draw your semi-circle, mark half-way along the long edge of the card. Tie about 10 inches (25 cm) of string to a pencil. Hold down the end of the string with your finger on the mark. Pull the string tight and draw a semi-circle.

2. Roll the card stock into a cone shape, leaving a small opening at the narrow end. Tape the edges together.

3. Attach a strip of card stock to the underside of the cone to make a handle and decorate the cone with pens or paints (or glue on some colored shapes).

4. Put the ear trumpet to your ear to hear quiet sounds louder. Speak through the cone and turn it into a **megaphone** to make your voice sound louder.

NEAR AND FAR

The further away you are from a **sound source**, the quieter it sounds. The nearer you are, the louder it sounds. You can tell roughly how far away something is by how loud it sounds.

Thunder

When a thunderstorm is a few miles away, you see the flash of lightning seconds before you hear the crash of thunder. This is because sound travels at about 1,087 feet (331 m) per second, more slowly than light, which travels at about 186,000 miles (300,000 km) per second.

When a thunderstorm is overhead, you hear thunder and you see lightning at almost the same time.

Sound spreads out

At an airport, a passenger jet sounds very loud when it takes off! When the jet is high in the air, you can hardly hear it from the ground. This is because the sound waves have spread out and the sound is faint by the time it reaches your ears. People who work close to noisy sounds often wear ear coverings to protect their ears.

This worker is wearing safety earmuffs because they are close to a noisy drill.

ACTIVITY

MAKE A STETHOSCOPE

Ask an adult to help you with this activity.

You will need:

- **long cardboard tube**
- **2 paper cups**
- **tape**

1. Ask an adult to cut the narrow end off each of the paper cups.

2. Tape the narrow end of each cup to either end of the tube to make your stethoscope.

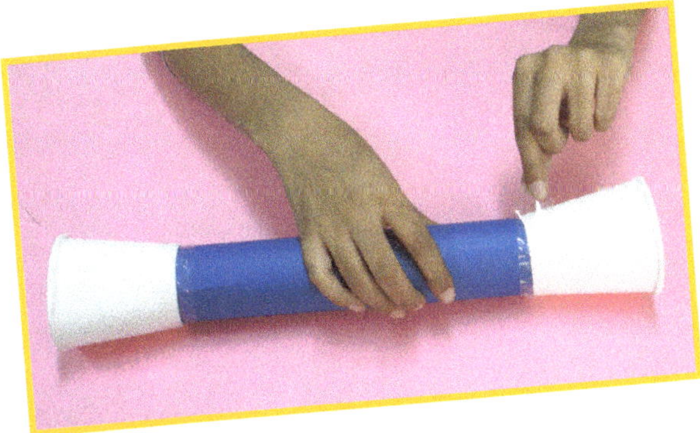

3. Put one end of the stethoscope onto your friend's chest, near to their heart. Put your ear to the other end of the stethoscope to listen to your friend's heartbeat. How fast is the heart beating? What other faint sounds can you hear?

Doctors use stethoscopes to listen to sounds inside our body. A stethoscope makes quiet noises sound louder and nearer.

BOUNCING SOUND

Sound bounces off surfaces like a ball bouncing off a wall. This is called reflection. Sound waves bounce off hard, smooth surfaces in one direction. They bounce off rough surfaces in different directions.

The walls of a recording studio are lined with materials that absorb sound.

Muffled!

When sounds hit a soft surface they are absorbed (or taken in). Noises can be **muffled** and made quieter with soft, absorbent material. Thick curtains in your bedroom help to muffle any outside sounds and give you a peaceful night's sleep.

Echo

If you stand in a large, empty room and shout your name, you will hear it repeated back to you as an echo. The sound of your voice reflects off the walls back into your ears. You don't hear an echo in a small room full of furniture.

In empty spaces, such as caves and canyons, you can hear your voice as an echo.

ACTIVITY

MAKE AN ECHO CATCHER

You will need:

- **cutting board**
- **pile of books**
- **2 long cardboard tubes**
- **colored paper**
- **glue or tape**
- **pens or paints**
- **sound source (such as a ticking clock or wind-up toy)**
- **kitchen towel**
- **sheet of corrugated cardboard**

1. Use the books to prop up the cutting board on a table, to make a vertical "wall."

2. Wrap the cardboard tubes in colored paper and decorate them. Lie the tubes on the table in a V-shape with the point of the V close to the cutting board.

3. Put the sound source at the end of one tube and your ear to the end of the other. You will hear the sound as it travels down one tube, reflects off the hard board and back along the other tube. What you hear is an echo.

4. Hang the kitchen towel over the cutting board and try again. Now replace the cutting board with the corrugated cardboard. Can you still hear the echo?

MUSICAL SOUNDS

Musicians in an orchestra pluck, scrape, blow, bang, and rattle their instruments to make musical sounds. The conductor brings in the different instruments and shows the musicians how fast or slow to play.

A small, metal triangle hit with a metal beater makes a high, tinkling sound.

Vibrating air

Musical sounds are caused by air vibrating around and inside an instrument. Air vibrates along the tubes of a trombone and inside a violin, for example. The shape, size, and material the instrument is made from give it a particular sound.

Pieces of music are written for different types of instruments to play together.

Stringed instruments

Stringed instruments are plucked with fingers or scraped with a bow. The strings vibrate and air inside the instrument vibrates to make the sound louder. Thick strings vibrate slowly and make a low sound. Thin strings vibrate quickly and make a higher sound.

A violin has four strings. Each has a different thickness.

ACTIVITY

MAKE A STRINGED INSTRUMENT

You will need:

- **empty tissue box**
- **pens (or glue and colored paper)**
- **3 long rubber bands of different widths**
- **2 pencils**

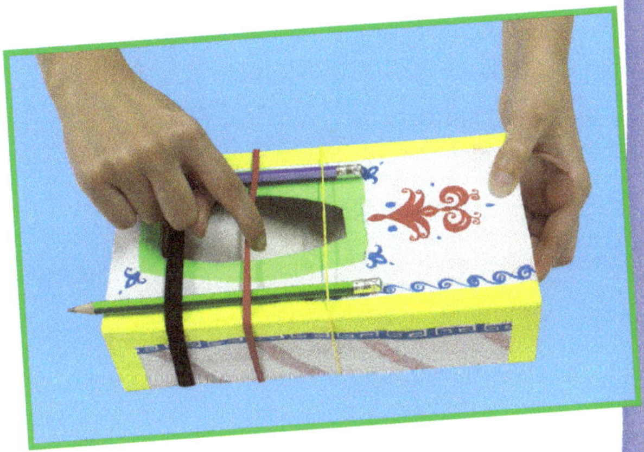

1. Decorate your tissue box with pens or colored paper. Stretch the rubber bands around the tissue box. Make sure they run over the hole.

2. Push the pencils under the elastic bands at each side of the box. Pluck the bands between the pencils. Watch them vibrate and hear the different sounds they make.

3. Move the pencils towards the middle of the box to shorten the bands between the pencils, or towards the edges of the box to lengthen them. How can you make a very high or low sound?

CHANGING SOUNDS

You can change musical sounds and make them higher and lower or louder and quieter. Volume is how loud or quiet a sound is. Pitch is how high or low a sound is.

Some opera singers are trained to reach very high notes with their voice.

Volume

Musicians make the sound of an instrument louder by blowing, scraping, or hitting harder. They make the sound quieter by playing the instrument more gently. A loud sound makes big vibrations and a quiet sound makes smaller vibrations.

Instruments can be played loudly or quietly. The padded ends of drumsticks help to make a soft, quiet sound, if needed.

Pitch

The pitch of a **note** changes when its vibrations become faster or slower. Players play different notes by changing the length of the string (or tube of air) of their instruments.

A xylophone can produce different pitches (or notes). The larger keys are lower notes, while the smaller keys are higher notes.

ACTIVITY

MAKE A TUNED WIND INSTRUMENT

You will need:

- **plastic bottles of different sizes**
- **large jug of water colored with food coloring**
- **pencil**

1. Pour some water into one of the bottles. Practice blowing across the open bottle top to make the air inside it vibrate and play a note. Alternatively, tap the bottle lightly with a pencil.

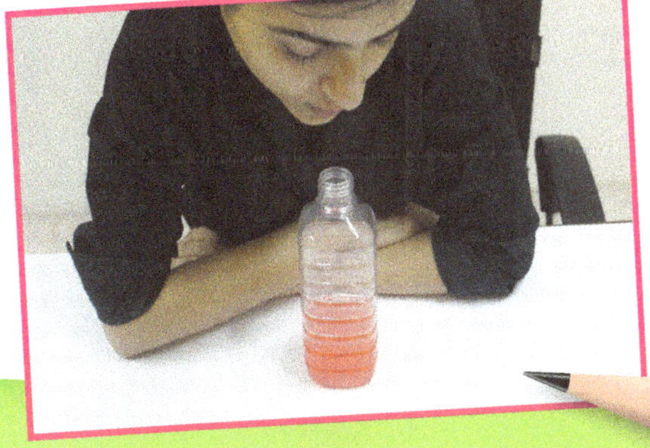

2. Experiment with the amount of water and size of the bottle to play notes of different pitches.

3. Arrange the bottles in order from low notes on the left to the highest note on the right.

You now have a tuned wind instrument!

ULTRASOUND

Sound that is too high for us to hear is called ultrasound. Even though we can't hear ultrasound, we can use it in all kinds of different ways.

Ultrasound can be used to measure the depth of ocean water.

Sound pictures

Ultrasound is used to make pictures of things that we wouldn't normally be able to see, such as an unborn baby or a shipwreck on the bottom of the ocean. Ultrasound waves are sent out and reflected off the object. These echoes are shown as a picture on a screen.

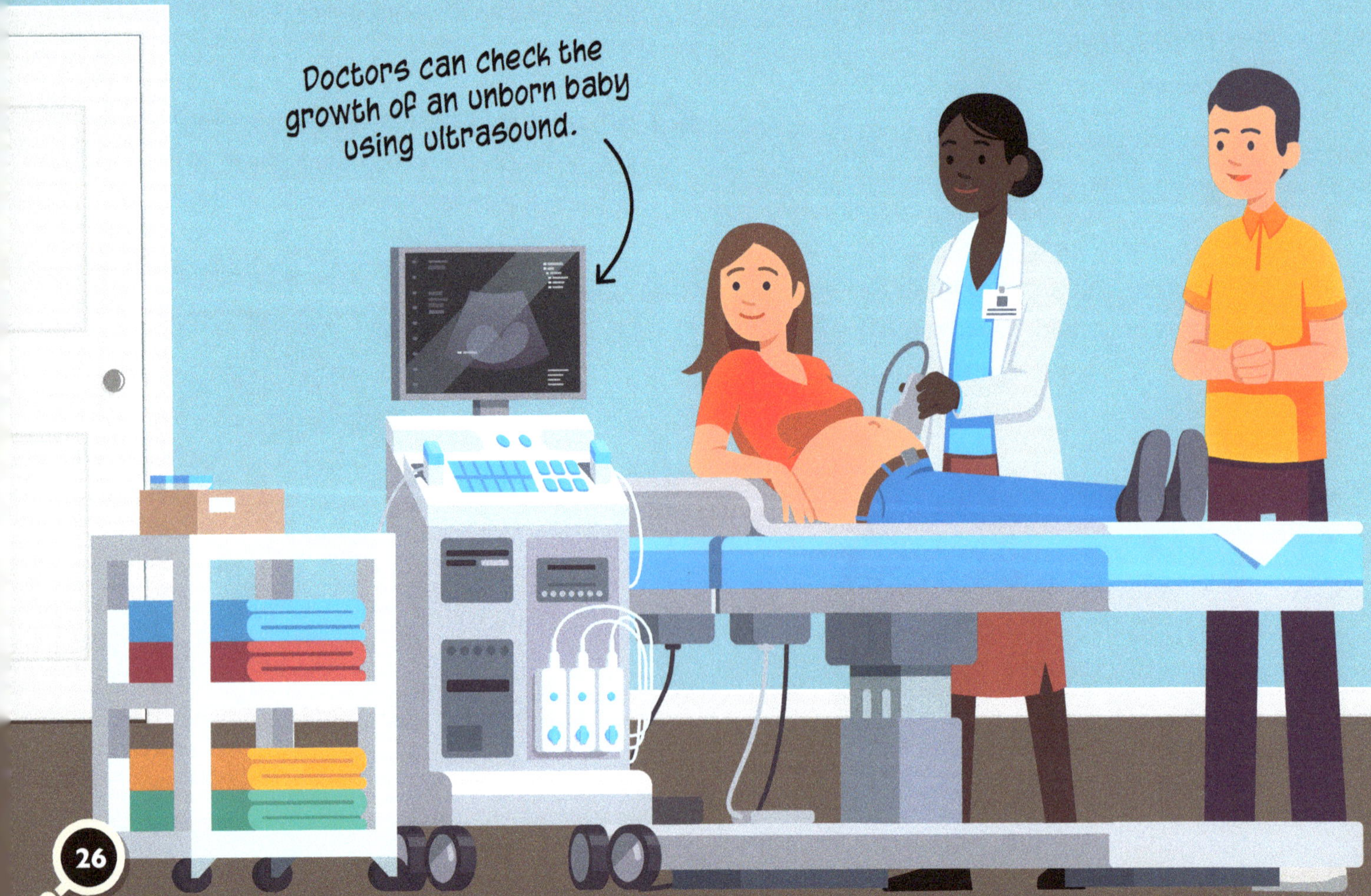

Doctors can check the growth of an unborn baby using ultrasound.

Cleaning

Ultrasound can be used for cleaning small, delicate objects. Ultrasound waves vibrate a mixture of water and cleaning solution to remove dirt without causing damage.

Silent whistles

Dogs can hear much higher sounds than we can. Dog owners use "dog whistles" with an ultrasonic sound to give their dog orders that only they can hear.

ACTIVITY

RESEARCH USES OF ULTRASOUND

You will need:

- **sheet of paper**
- **ruler**
- **pencil or pen**
- **reference books**
- **computer**

1. Draw a chart like the one here. Use books and the internet to find information about ultrasound and its different uses.

2. Write notes and draw pictures about what ultrasound can do. Some have been added for you, but there are others too.

Use	Application	How they work	Picture
Medical procedures	Monitoring an unborn baby Finding out causes of pain or swelling		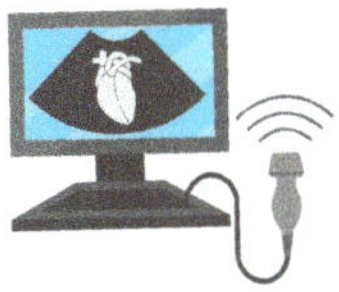
Dentistry	Toothbrush	Ultrasonic toothbrush vibrates fluid in your mouth to help remove food and bacteria.	
Cleaning	Cleaning jewelery		
Detecting faults	Finding cracks in walls and pipes		
Measuring distance	Finding the depth of water		
Training dogs	Giving dog a command		

Glossary

adapted

A plant or animal that has adapted has changed (over millions of years) to suit its surroundings.

cochlea

The cochlea is part of the inner ear shaped like a snail shell. Sound waves pass through fluid in the cochlea.

communicate

When people and animals communicate, they give each other information by speaking, making sounds, or sending signals.

conductor

A conductor is the person in charge of an orchestra. The conductor signals when to play loudly or quietly, or faster or slower.

ear canal

The ear canal is found just behind the outer ear. Sound waves pass along this tunnel to the inner ear.

eardrum

The eardrum is at the end of the ear canal. It is a piece of skin that vibrates like a drum when sound waves hit it.

echo

An echo happens when sound waves bounce back at you off a hard surface and you hear the same sound twice.

gas

Gases are materials that have no shape. They spread out because the molecules are not held together.

liquid

A liquid is a material that flows and pours because the molecules are held loosely together.

megaphone

A megaphone is a device shaped like a cone that makes your voice sound louder.

molecules

Molecules are the smallest possible amount of a particular kind of matter that has all the characteristics of that matter.

muffled

Sound is muffled when it is made quieter.

note

A note is a sound of a particular pitch, either sung or played on a musical instrument.

pitch

The pitch of a note is how high or low it sounds.

predators

Animals that are predators hunt other animals for food.

prey

Animals that are prey are hunted by other animals for food.

reflection

Reflection happens when sound bounces off a hard surface.

solid

A solid is a material that can hold its shape because the molecules are packed closely together.

sound source

A sound source makes a sound.

sound waves

Sound travels through the air in sound waves. Sound waves are made when air vibrates.

ultrasound

Ultrasonic sound (ultrasound) is too high for us to hear.

vibrations

Vibrations are very small, fast movements to and fro.

vocal cords

Your vocal cords are in your throat. They vibrate and produce sounds when air passes through them.

volume

The volume of a sound is how loud or quiet it is.

Quiz

1 Big vibrations make:

a) loud sounds
b) quiet sounds
c) high sounds
d) low sounds

2 Sound travels fastest in:

a) solids
b) liquids
c) gases
d) space

3 Ears are shaped to:

a) keep you balanced
b) keep you cool
c) keep out flies
d) catch sound waves

4 Your ear has:

a) two tiny bones
b) three tiny bones
c) four tiny bones
d) five tiny bones

5 Bats have big ears to:

a) help them fly
b) balance in trees
c) hunt in the daytime
d) hunt in the dark

6 In air, sound travels at about:

a) 1,086 feet per second
b) 10,860 feet per second
c) 186 feet per second
d) 86 feet per second

7 Hard, smooth surfaces cause sound waves to:

a) reflect in one direction
b) reflect in two directions
c) reflect in different directions
d) become absorbed

8 A big instrument usually makes:

a) a loud sound
b) a quiet sound
c) a low sound
d) a high sound

9. **On an instrument, thick strings vibrate:**

a) quickly to make a high sound
b) quickly to make a low sound
c) slowly to make a high sound
d) slowly to make a low sound

10. **Sounds that are too high for us to hear are called:**

a) ultraviolet
b) ultrasound
c) ultramarine
d) ultrafiche

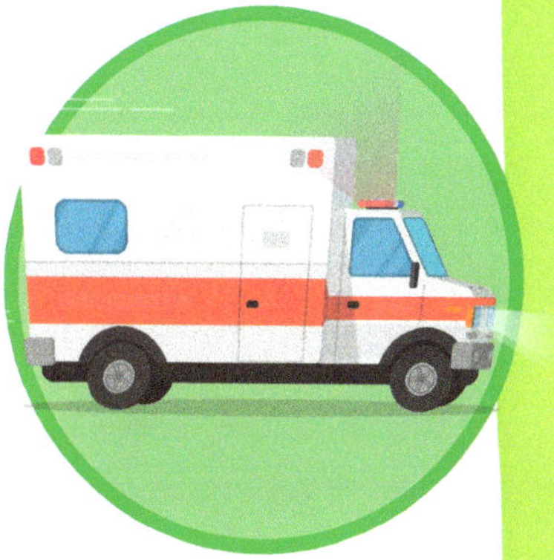

ANSWERS 1a, 2a, 3d, 4b, 5d, 6a, 7a, 8c, 9d, 10b

FURTHER INFORMATION

BOOKS

A Question of Science: Can you hear sounds in space? by Anna Claybourne, Wayland

Boom Science: Sound by Georgia Amson-Bradshaw, Franklin Watts

Extreme Science: Spectacular Light and Sound by Jon Richards, Wayland

Science in a Flash: Sound by Georgia Amson-Bradshaw, Franklin Watts

WEBSITES

All about sound and vibrations: www.bbc.co.uk/bitesize/topics/zgffr82

Listen to learn more about sound waves: www.funkidslive.com/learn/waves/sound-waves

Try your hand at some sound experiments: www.fizzicseducation.com.au/category/150-science-experiments/light-sound-experiments

Find out more and test yourself: www.dkfindout.com/uk/science/sound

Index